To my mother,
whose roots are my roots
and who taught me the value of sharing.

S. D.

For Alec.
The moon is beautiful, isn't it? x

H. H.

PUFFIN BOOKS

UK | USA | Canada | Ireland | Australia
India | New Zealand | South Africa

Puffin Books is part of the Penguin Random House group of companies whose addresses can be found at global.penguinrandomhouse.com.

www.penguin.co.uk   www.puffin.co.uk   www.ladybird.co.uk

First published 2025

001

Text copyright © Susie Dent, 2025
Illustrations copyright © Harriet Hobday, 2025

The moral right of the author and illustrator has been asserted

No part of this book may be used or reproduced in any manner for the purpose of training artificial intelligence technologies or systems. In accordance with Article 4(3) of the DSM Directive 2019/790, Penguin Random House expressly reserves this work from the text and data mining exception.

Text design by Sally Griffin
Printed and bound in China

The authorized representative in the EEA is Penguin Random House Ireland, Morrison Chambers, 32 Nassau Street, Dublin D02 YH68

A CIP catalogue record for this book is available from the British Library

ISBN: 978-0-241-71782-0

Penguin Random House is committed to a sustainable future for our business, our readers and our planet. This book is made from Forest Stewardship Council® certified paper.

The ROOTS we SHARE

100 WORDS THAT BRING US TOGETHER

FROM BRITAIN'S BEST-LOVED WORD EXPERT

SUSIE DENT

illustrated by Harriet Hobday

PUFFIN

INTRODUCTION

As I write this introduction, sitting at my desk, my rescue cat Bo is snuggling happily on my lap. While she purrs away softly, she reminds me once again of the company and love she gives me, which I also try to give to her. She is one of the many connections in my life that make me happy. And she is also one of the reasons I decided to write a book about togetherness.

When we think of the word 'together', we probably think of our families, friends and pets, who we connect with regularly. They are all important to our happiness and well-being. But there are many other things that connect us deeply to the world we live in and to one another. In *The Roots We Share*,

I have set out to explore some of the ways in which every one of us fits into this world, like individual pieces in a giant jigsaw.

There is a popular saying that I think holds an important lesson. It tells us that 'there is more that unites us than divides us'. It reminds me that even when we are fighting, or in disagreement – or even at war – we all have a lot more in common than we think. For example, we each want to feel safe and at peace, to be healthy and to look after our loved ones. We also all appreciate beauty, whatever that might mean to us.

Sometimes it's easy to forget the many things we share with others. So I have set out to find 100 words that bring us together, because language really can remind us how closely connected we all are.

I begin with 'kindness', one of the most powerful forms of connection. It is a word with an ancient past, but with a very simple meaning. One small act of kindness can have a ripple effect that then spreads to a whole community. By sharing a kind act with someone else, from a smile to a helping hand, we are passing along hope and love, which they in turn might pass on to others.

Music also offers another important way of connecting with others, even when we don't speak the same language. When we sing a song or listen to its rhythm, we become part of a whole community of people who have enjoyed this song too, sometimes across entire generations.

The story of food is also the story of connection. It goes back so much further than the shop where we bought our ingredients. From the seeds that turned into vegetables to the gardeners who planted them; from the sunshine and rain that helped them grow to the workers who harvested them, food connects us to our environment and to others. It would be hard to find a nicer way of sharing conversations and laughter than over a lovely meal.

That connection to the natural world is vital to our well-being. If you've ever been lucky enough to walk in a forest on a cloudless day, you may notice rays of sunshine breaking through the trees above and dancing on the woodland floor. Whenever I see this dappled light, even when I'm on my own, I feel a deep sense of peace and calm, and this reminds me of the importance of nature. The animals that roam the world, the insects we see in our gardens and the trees that help us breathe: every one of these things gives something back to the world they share with us.

We also have a large vocabulary with which to express love and friendship, which makes us feel part of something bigger than ourselves. It has been proven that our relationships with others make us happier and healthier. Whether it's the bond we share with family and friends or the communities we belong to, this feeling of togetherness can be found in many different places.

And what better way to bond with others than through laughter? You don't need to speak someone else's language to share a smile with them. Laughter is infectious: when we see someone else having fun, we automatically feel a little better ourselves. This is a different kind of language that unites us all.

It is of course true that laughter isn't always possible. Sometimes it can be hard to hold on to hope when sad things are happening around us. When I open my dictionary (the most magical of books!), I often notice that our language is full of negative words. But I also know that if I look a little

longer, I will find a word that makes me smile or that reminds me of something happy. For example, I can't see or hear the word 'waddle' without a chuckle! It immediately takes me to a happy thought: the wobbly walk of a group of penguins. And that is the power of words. When it feels like hope, harmony, happiness or peace are too far away, words can remind us of the possibility of joy, unity and connection.

Words have the power to calm us too. To open a book is to enter a world that can be very different from our own, one full of adventures and magic that can soothe the stresses of our day and allow us a special kind of harmony. Feeling at peace with ourselves is every bit as important as finding it in the world.

I hope that by reading the words in this book and enjoying their bright, beautiful illustrations, you will discover new ways to think and learn. Here you will find the story of unfamiliar words such as 'twitter-light' and 'conjobble', as well as some you might already know, such as 'ocean' and 'friend'. You will find words from other languages too, which remind us that although the world is vast, we all live alongside each other within it. Most of all, I hope that these stories of the roots we share help you reflect on the importance of togetherness, love and friendship, as well as kindness and hope. Perhaps, bit by bit, through the power of these words, we can remind ourselves of the many things that unite us all.

Susie Dent

KINDNESS

'Kind' is a word with many meanings. In Old English, 'kind' described a person's inner nature, formed at birth. The word is a relative of 'king', because good manners were expected from those of noble birth. Over time, 'kind' came to mean generous and considerate, as we know it today. Within every meaning of this special word is the sense that being kind towards others is an essential part of being human.

ALTRUISM

Altruism is the kind and selfless desire to help other people, while expecting nothing in return.

KINDNESS | 1

SIMPATICO

English borrowed the word 'simpatico' from Spanish and Italian to describe someone who is friendly, cheerful and easy to get along with.

MENSCH

The language of Yiddish, once spoken by many Jewish people in central and eastern Europe, is still used in Israel and parts of Europe and the USA today. Many of its words, such as 'bagel', have happily settled in English. Lots of them have a very pleasing sound. 'Schnozz' (the nose), 'schlep' (to move with great effort) and 'schmooze' (to chat with people and try to charm them) all come from Yiddish. As does the word 'mensch', used to describe a very special type of person who is honest and kind, and who always looks out for other people.

Do you know someone who you would call a mensch?

GOODWILLY

Reading some of the words in a dictionary can certainly make you smile, and 'goodwilly' is one of them! In the eighteenth century this word meant 'full of affection or good intention'. If you were a goodwilly kind of person, you were kind, generous and cheerful. Anyone who was bad-tempered and unkind, on the other hand, was known as 'ill-willy' or, worse, 'evil-willy'!

ATONE

When we atone for something, we admit we have made a mistake and wish to make up for it. We might, for example, atone for being unkind to someone by saying how sorry we are. If you split the word up, you will see that it consists of two words: 'at' and 'one'. When we atone for a mistake, we are reunited with the person we hurt and become 'at one' again.

KINDNESS

5

MUSIC

Music makes our lives richer in so many ways. It is one of the most powerful means we have of uniting with others. It is a bridge between different people and cultures and is almost a language by itself: one that everyone can understand.

'Music' is also a word with a wonderful history. The ancient Greeks had a large collection of tales about gods, goddesses and epic heroes, and these stories helped them explain and understand the world. In Greek, *mousikē* described the art of the Muses, the nine goddesses who were believed to inspire all learning and creativity. Legend told how anyone who heard the Muses sing would instantly forget their troubles.

TARAB

'Tarab' comes from the Arabic language. It describes a lively, rhythmic style of folk music, and the way such music can enchant its listeners, who instantly fall under its spell. At the heart of the word is a deep appreciation of the power of music, and the intense emotions that it inspires, uniting the audience and the musician.

GLEE-DREAM

This word, from Old English, once described the very special kind of happiness we feel when we listen to music. 'Dream' meant something very different then: it described merriment and celebration, while the word 'glee' described entertainment and play. Put the two ideas together and you end up with something very joyful indeed.

KARAOKE

Do you enjoy singing with your friends around a microphone? Or perhaps you've even had a go at karaoke, taking it in turns with other people to perform your favourite song as the lyrics bounce across the screen in front of you? The word 'karaoke' comes from Japanese, where it means 'empty orchestra', because the music is played on a backing track rather than by live musicians. The most important sound is our voice as we sing along.

CONCERT

Many of us dream about going to the concert of our favourite singer or band. Some of us may have taken part in a concert ourselves, by singing or playing a musical instrument. The word 'concert' describes a musical performance given in public. Its story is all about bringing voices and people together, because at its heart is the Italian word *concertare*, meaning 'to harmonize'.

SYMPHONY

A symphony is a musical piece that is usually written for a full orchestra. You can also use this word to describe different things uniting in a beautiful way, such as symphonies of colour dancing together as they meet in a painting. It began with Greek, in which *sumphōnia* meant 'together sound' – a beautiful way of talking about music from instruments that combine in perfect harmony.

Did you know that 'symphony' is a relative of the word 'telephone', a word that means 'sound from far away' because we use it to speak to people who are at a distance from us?

COMMUNITY

There is a lot of evidence to show that being part of a community is central to our happiness, bringing us feelings of safety, support and understanding. Community is all about belonging. It describes a group of people who are living in the same place or who have something in common and are united by shared values. Being in a community gives us a sense of being part of something bigger than ourselves.

KIN

'Kin' is an old word for our family and relations. It appears in 'kindred', meaning 'related' or 'similar in kind'. When we make a connection with someone and discover that their attitudes and values are very similar to ours, we might say they are our 'kindred spirit'.

TRADITION

Bedtime stories, pizza nights, hanging up a Christmas stocking, giving gifts for Hanukkah or sharing meals at Eid: these are all traditions that might belong to your family or your community. A tradition is a custom or belief that is handed down from generation to generation over many years. They are valuable in giving us a sense of connection and a feeling of continuity between past and present.

The literal meaning of 'tradition' is 'handing over', from the Latin *trans*, meaning 'across', and *dare*, 'to give'.

LA PASSEGGIATA

Every country and culture has its own customs and traditions. In Italy, an afternoon rest is often followed by *una passeggiata*, which translates as 'a walk', but it is also so much more than that.

This tradition involves an evening stroll around a town or village during which everyone greets each other as they pass by, or stops to talk and catch up.

Everyone takes part: young people, old people, families and individuals. A *passeggiata* makes each person feel included and part of the community.

DEMOCRACY

'Democracy' is an important word. It means 'rule by the people'. It is up to the people of a democratic country to decide how it is run, or to elect representatives to make these decisions for them. At its heart are the Greek words *dēmos*, 'the people', and *kratia*, meaning 'power' or 'rule'.

In a democracy, citizens can have their say by voting. This comes from Latin, in which a *votum* is a promise or wish. When we vote as part of a democracy, we are promising our support for a person or decision.

SHALOM AND SALAAM

In many cultures and religions, traditional greetings involve a blessing or wish. In Arabic-speaking and Muslim countries, for example, *salaam* is a shortening of the Arabic *al-salām alaikum*, meaning 'peace be upon you'. Similarly, a greeting between Jewish people upon meeting is *shalom*, which comes from the Hebrew *šālōm*, meaning 'peace'. A wish for harmony and compassion runs through each of these greetings.

ALOHA

Hello, hi, hola, ciao, hey, howdy... how many ways do you know of greeting someone when you meet them? In Hawaii, a traditional hello is 'aloha', which also means love, friendship and compassion.

COLLOQUIAL

Talking is one of the most important ways of connecting with others. A 'colloquy' is a conversation: an exchange between two people who take it in turns to speak. And if you are speaking 'colloquially', you might be using slang, an informal language that binds a group together and makes each member feel that they belong.

HEARKEN

Good conversation is as much about listening as speaking. When we say something that feels important to us, we hope that others hear what we are saying, even if they disagree. In Anglo-Saxon times, people talked about 'hearkening', which meant listening attentively and respectfully to another person. It is a sibling of the word 'hark' that you find in the Christmas carol 'Hark! The Herald Angels Sing'.

NATURE

Nature is the essence of everything. It is at the heart of who we are (our 'human nature') and of the world we live in, from the sea and the mountains to the animals and plants around us. The word comes from the Latin *natus*, meaning 'born'. Nature is about the living things in our world, and so it feels fitting that its name focuses on birth and growth, the natural cycle of life.

KOMOREBI

Have you ever been lucky enough to walk through a wood or forest on a sunny day? Perhaps you can picture the sunlight filtering through the canopy of trees above you. The Japanese word *komorebi* describes the magical sight of sunshine breaking through the trees and dancing upon the woodland floor. It is a word that expresses a deep connection with nature and becoming immersed in our surroundings.

The movement of shadows and light that we see in *komorebi* can also remind us of how life is constantly changing, and how darkness will always eventually turn to light.

MOONGLADE

Few things are more special than looking at a full moon. When moonlight is reflected on the surface of the sea or a lake it can make a glowing track across the water. This is known by the glittering name of 'moonglade'.

The Moon appears in unexpected places in English. Monday was originally 'Moon-Day', because days of the week in ancient Rome were named after the planets, which at the time were believed to include the Sun and the Moon. You can also find it in the word 'month', as we used to track the changing months by the cycle of the Moon.

TWITTER-LIGHT

Centuries ago, 'twitter-light' described the hours around dusk that seem to hover between night and day, when the Sun has set but night has yet to fall. 'Twitter' here refers to the gentle tweeting of birds that we can hear just before darkness descends. Today, we use the word 'twilight', in which 'twi' means 'two', because these are the hours between two periods: night and day.

GLIMMER-GOWK

The sight of an owl swooping across a night sky is as rare as it is majestic. And while the word 'owl' covers many species, from the barn owl to the screech owl and the church owl to the brown owl, there is just one word from Lincolnshire in England that beautifully captures the effect of the bird's wings as it glides silently above us. This is the 'glimmer-gowk', referring to the soft light that reflects off an owl's wings in the moonlight.

FRILUFTSLIV

Spending time outdoors can give us a chance to pause and let our minds and bodies reset, especially when life becomes too busy. In the Norwegian language, the word *friluftsliv* reflects the value of spending time outside. It translates into English as 'open-air living' and describes a life in which nature is cherished and appreciated for its beauty.

PACIFIC

The Pacific Ocean is the largest and deepest ocean on Earth, encompassing over 60 million square miles. Its name is just as meaningful, as 'pacific' means 'peaceful'. When explorers in the sixteenth century emerged from a stretch of water known for its choppiness, they entered an ocean that felt calm and tranquil, inspiring the name 'peaceful ocean'.

OCEAN

The word 'ocean' itself also tells a story. The ancient Greeks believed the world was surrounded by one huge body of water, which they called *okeanos*. 'Ocean' originally described what was thought to be this 'Great Outer Sea' with waves that washed around the disc of the entire Earth. Meanwhile, the name of the Mediterranean is based on the Latin for sea 'in the middle of the Earth'.

PHILOCALY

When you hear the word 'beauty', what do you think of? It might be a fiery sunset that lights up the sky, a dress with a colour that sings to you in a special way, a flower boldly poking its head through some weeds or an extraordinary goal that almost defies belief. We all find beauty in different things. 'Philocaly' describes a love of beauty, including the kind that can be found in the smallest things. And if you are someone who finds beauty everywhere in life, then you can call yourself a 'philocalist'!

FOOD

When people come together for a meal, they share an experience that involves much more than eating. They bond over cooking, conversation and enjoying each other's company.

The word 'food' is over 1,000 years old, but it is not the oldest word in English for the things we eat and drink. Before this, we used the word 'meat' for all food, not just the kind that comes from animals. Vegetables were known as 'green meat', and milk and other dairy foods were called 'white meat'. 'Food' eventually took over to describe all these different things. Have you had your green meat today?!

FIKA

Sharing food with people is a special thing. It might be taking turns to break off a piece of chocolate with a friend in the park, sharing popcorn in the cinema or having dinner around a table. Food brings us together; it is a wonderful way to relax and connect with the important people in our lives. In Sweden, they have a word for meeting up with a friend and enjoying food together. *Fika* means taking a break and chatting over coffee and cake.

FOOD | 31

SOBREMESA

Sometimes, we lead such busy lives that we don't take enough time over a meal, quickly wolfing down breakfast before dashing off, or guzzling down dinner so we can leave the table. When we do eat, we might also be looking at our phones or watching TV. All of this can mean we often don't take the time to really savour our food and enjoy the company of the people we're eating with.

In Spanish-speaking countries, the time spent sitting around a table and talking to people, even after a meal has finished, is known as *sobremesa*. It translates to 'over the table', because it is all about relaxing at the dining table with loved ones, sharing food and stories from the day and spending quality time together.

PICNIC

Imagine a blanket laid out on the grass, covered with delicious sandwiches, mini pies, strawberries and cupcakes: is there anything nicer than a picnic with friends or family? Today's picnics tend to be very relaxed, a way of enjoying the sunshine and having fun outdoors, but 300 years ago they were very fashionable parties to which every guest brought some food. Stories and paintings tell of grand picnics being held at big country houses and enjoyed by people dressed in their smartest outfits.

We took 'picnic' from the French *pique-nique*, in which *piquer* means 'to pick' and *nique* was simply chosen for its rhyme. Can you think of similar rhyming words with two parts like this? Do you have lots of knick-knacks? Or perhaps you love wearing flip-flops while playing ping-pong or having a KitKat!

ONION

Onions have been part of the vegetable garden since medieval times. They may make us cry, but their name holds a rather beautiful image of unity and togetherness. Here's a clue: instead of saying 'un-yun', try saying 'one-yun' instead. The 'one', which in Latin is *unus*, was the inspiration for the onion's name, because an onion's layers come together to form one single unit, as opposed to the many separate cloves in a bulb of garlic, for example.

COMPANION

A companion is someone we spend time with, who keeps us company on our adventures and who shares our interests. In the past, a companion shared one specific thing: food. The root of the word lies in the Latin *com*, which means 'together with', and *panis*, meaning 'bread'. A companion was someone who sat alongside us and shared our bread.

The link between friendship and food can be seen in the word 'mate', too, because it is a very close relative of 'meat'.

CONJOBBLE

In the seventeenth century, getting together for a good chat with someone over some food was called 'conjobbling'. When you say it aloud, doesn't it bring to mind a special scene of a group of friends munching away on delicious food, while sharing funny stories?

LOVE

Love comes in so many different forms. Our love for our parents is not the same as the love we feel for our friends, and that is different again from the love we have for our pets. Each of these kinds of love will also change over time. The range of love we feel is enormous, and yet in English we use just one word to cover all of it.

BEARN-LUFU

A thousand years ago, people distinguished very carefully between different kinds of love. 'Bearn-lufu' was a mother's love for her child, 'sib-lufu' was the love of one's family, and 'freond-lufu' was 'friend-love'. Today, we rely on just a single word, 'love', to express them all, but its power is enormous. In fact, it would be hard to find another word that covers a greater range of feelings.

Are there other kinds of 'lufu' you think we should have a word for too?

KOI NO YOKAN

Have you ever heard the saying 'love at first sight'? It's when two people meet for the first time and know, straight away, that they love one another. In Japan, they describe a similar feeling, *koi no yokan*. This is when two people come together and know that, eventually, they will fall in love.

English has no word for this early moment in the journey of love – one that looks to a future that we know is bound to come.

TROTH

When two people decide to spend their lives with one another, they may choose to have a ceremony at which they promise to stay together. This promise is often made in the form of a vow, when the couple 'pledges' their 'troth', or gives their word to be there for each other for the rest of their lives. 'Troth' is a sibling of 'truth', and it survives in the word 'betrothed', which is the name used for the person you are engaged to before marriage.

ANTIPELARGY

'Antipelargy' describes a child's love for their parents. The story behind this word is very touching, for in ancient Greece the word *pelargos* was used for a stork. According to ancient legend, the long-legged wading bird carried its elderly parents on its wings. 'Antipelargy' came to mean the return of kindness: our parents look after us as we grow up, and we in turn care for them as they grow old.

FRIEND

Friends are the people who make us laugh more loudly, smile more brightly and live more happily. We have always needed them, and so it makes sense that the word is very old. Our oldest record of it appears in a famous poem from 1,200 years ago called *Beowulf*, in which a Danish prince fights a monster to save his people. In this epic tale, the king's great hall is described as filled with 'friends'. The beginnings of the word are older still, for it descends from an ancient root meaning simply 'to love'.

WYNN

Around 2,000 years ago an ancient writing system used letters that were known as runes. This word also meant a 'whisper' or 'secret', because runes were used in magic spells and rituals. Unlike our alphabet, where a letter represents only a sound, runes had names and shapes that held meanings. The rune 'wynn' was used for a 'w' sound. It was written as 'ᚹ', and was also used to illustrate joy, including the kind of joy that comes with love. The rune 'ᚹ' was eventually replaced by 'UU', which became our letter 'W' and which we still pronounce as 'double u'!

STOUND

Have you ever come across a smell, a song or a place that brings back a sudden memory of love and happiness? Perhaps it was a waft of perfume, the beginning of a song you used to love listening to on long journeys, or maybe an old photograph of somewhere you used to visit. This pang of emotion that can come out of nowhere was known in Old English as a 'stound', a momentary flash of connection with the past that can stop you in your tracks.

VALENTINE

Valentine's Day, on 14 February, is a celebration of love. There are many traditions associated with it, such as giving gifts of chocolates and flowers to your loved ones. Many people also exchange Valentine's cards containing a secret message or romantic poetry. The day was named after Saint Valentine, the patron of sweethearts. This is also where the verb 'to valentine' comes from, which was originally much more about birds than humans. It describes the calls that birds sing out to greet other birds and find a mate. When some birds, such as sparrows, barn owls and swans, find their partner, they often stay with them for life. There is even a 'lovebird': a very small African parrot that is famous for its affectionate behaviour. Who knew that birds could be so romantic!

HARMONY

Throughout history and across the world, there have been fights, wars and conflicts. Sometimes countries fight one another for land, sometimes the wars happen within a country and sometimes conflicts can take place very close to home. But when everyone comes together with compassion, calmness and unity, we are in harmony. Being in harmony with others is about being at peace with them and in total agreement.

In a musical harmony, instruments or voices unite to produce a joyful sound. At the heart of the word is the Greek *harmos*, meaning a 'joint', the part of something that connects it to another. The idea is of individual pieces coming together to form a perfect whole.

HARMONY

ARMISTICE

An armistice is a formal agreement made between enemies to stop fighting. It's for this reason that the day on which the First World War ended, 11 November 1918, was called Armistice Day. Today in the UK, we celebrate it as Remembrance Day, while in the US it is known as Veterans Day. 'Armistice' itself means the 'stopping of arms', because those who are at war put down their weapons and reach for peace.

CONCORD

'Concord' describes harmony between groups of people. Its origins are as simple as they are beautiful. The word is made up of two parts: the Latin *con*, which means 'with', and *cord*, which means 'heart'. Those who reach 'concord' are of one heart. The word is a relative of 'accord', meaning 'agreement', as well as the musical instrument the 'accordion', which produces harmonious and pleasing notes (at least when it is played well!).

PHILANTHROPY

Philanthropy is the desire to help other people. It means being charitable and supportive towards our fellow humans. Those who are able to might donate to a food bank, for example, or volunteer at a care home. They are being philanthropic by showing love and concern for others. These ideas are both hidden in the origin of the word, which comes from the Greek *philein*, 'to love', and *anthrōpos*, 'human being'. When we demonstrate philanthropy, we are showing selfless love towards others.

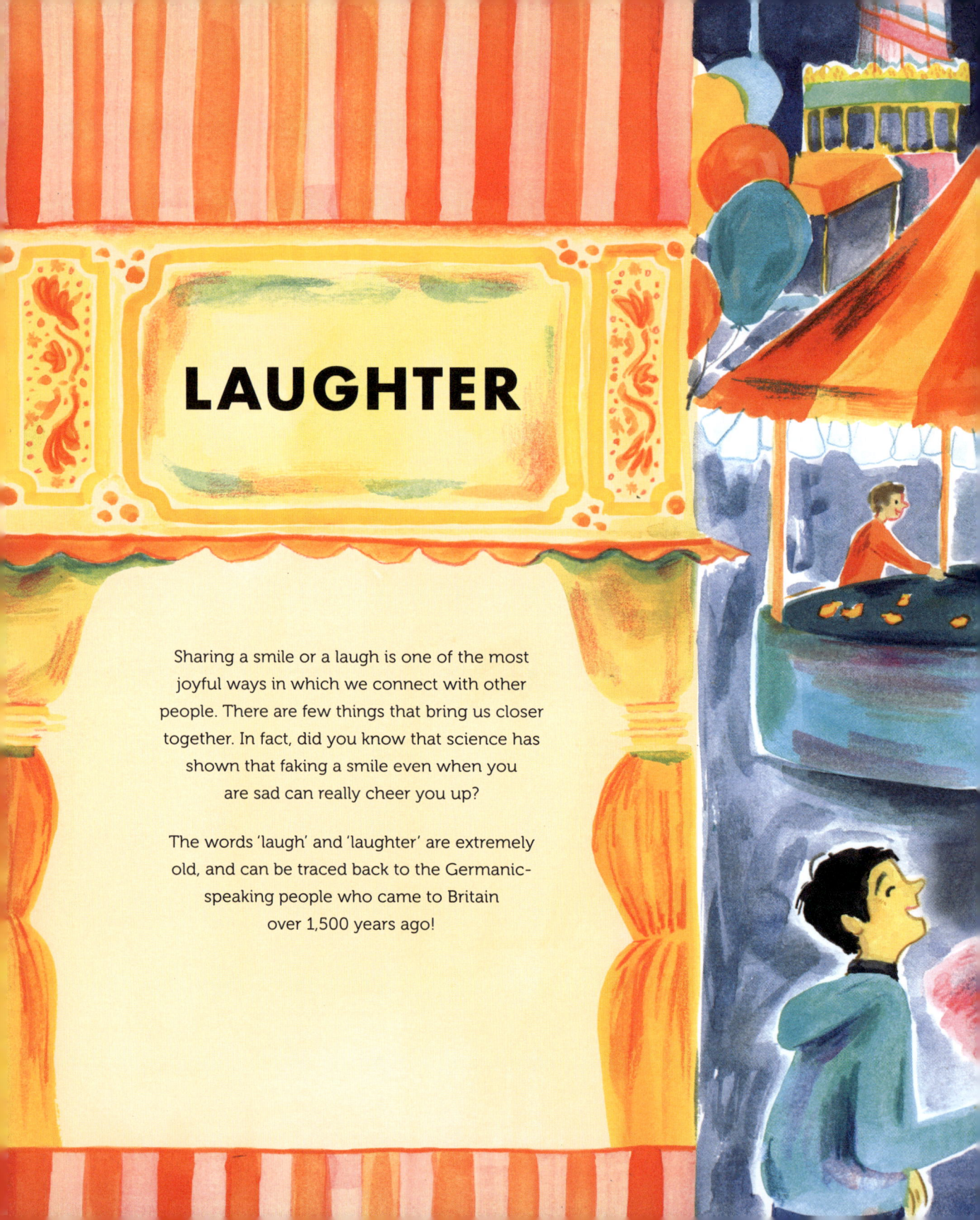

LAUGHTER

Sharing a smile or a laugh is one of the most joyful ways in which we connect with other people. There are few things that bring us closer together. In fact, did you know that science has shown that faking a smile even when you are sad can really cheer you up?

The words 'laugh' and 'laughter' are extremely old, and can be traced back to the Germanic-speaking people who came to Britain over 1,500 years ago!

CRAIC

At the heart of the word 'craic' is the idea of conversation, entertainment and laughter. To have 'good craic' is to have a really fun time. It comes from the medieval word 'crack', meaning 'loud talk', and is today used particularly in Ireland, where asking 'What's the craic?' is the same as asking 'What's up?' and describing someone as 'great craic' is like saying they are good company.

LAUGHTER

GELASTIC

Look in the mirror and pull the biggest smile you can. You might not know it, but you are exercising your gelastic muscles! The adjective 'gelastic' comes from Greek and describes things that make us smile and laugh.

COMEDY

Comedy is an ancient art form designed to make people laugh. These days you might watch comedians on TV, but in ancient Greece, comedy was performed at big festivals that were held in honour of the god Dionysus. Often it involved a play with a happy ending or a poem that was sung at a festive parade. The word is based on the Greek for 'revel singer', in which 'revel' means entertainment and enjoyment.

PUN

Why couldn't the pony sing in the choir?
Because he was a little horse.

What do you call an alligator in a vest?
An investigator!

These jokes rely on word play, and that is what puns are all about. A pun deliberately mixes up words that have the same sound or spelling as another word to produce something funny: 'horse' and 'hoarse', for example, sound the same. We don't know where the word 'pun' comes from, but we do know it is over 400 years old. Do you have a favourite pun?

FUN

The US gymnast and Olympic gold medallist Simone Biles once said, 'At the end of the day, if I can say I had fun, it was a good day.'

Having fun is so important, and it's something you can do on your own as well as with other people. At first this word was used to describe a prank played on someone, so even if it made some people laugh, it may not always have felt fun to the person being tricked! But over time 'fun' came to mean anything that is amusing and enjoyable for everyone. And, of course, it comes from the same family as 'funny'.

WEATHER

We love talking about the weather. In fact, it's estimated that most of us will spend a total of five months of our lives discussing it! But it is not just our conversations about the weather that bring us together: wherever we are in the world, we each experience the changing seasons and the feelings they can inspire. Whether it's cold or hot, rainy or misty, snowy or sweltering, and whether you're wrapping yourself up in a warm coat or standing beneath the pouring rain, we have lots of words to describe the ever-changing weather. Records of the word go back over 1,000 years, but its roots are older still, and it is likely to be from the same family as 'wind'.

DOG DAYS

'Dog days' might seem an odd name for the hottest period of the year, when life seems to slow down. Might it come from the idea that dogs always seek out the shade on stifling summer days?

The story behind this expression may surprise you, for the dog here is not one of our four-legged friends. It is a reference to Sirius, the brightest star in our night sky, which is also known as the 'dog star'. During the hottest part of summer in Mediterranean countries, Sirius the Dog Star is said to rise with the Sun. Sirius is part of the constellation known as Canis Major, the 'Great Dog'. According to a Greek legend, the Great Dog was an incredibly fast runner and had a race against a fox, which was thought to be the fastest creature on Earth. The dog won easily, and so the gods placed it among the stars to celebrate its victory.

WEATHER

CAT'S PAW

Imagine sitting on a riverbank and staring lazily at the water as insects such as dragonflies skim across it. Some insects, like water boatmen, seem to walk on the water as they move. When a wind or breeze ruffles the surface, beautiful patterns are formed. Sailors in the past noticed them and named the ripple effect of air as it blows across the smooth water 'cat's paw'. They imagined an invisible cat making tiny tracks across a river or sea.

PLUVIOPHILE

If you love splashing joyfully through puddles or standing beneath a welcome downpour of rain during the hot summer months, you could describe yourself as a 'pluviophile' – someone who savours rainy days.

ON CLOUD NINE

When we are 'on cloud nine' we are blissfully happy. The idea is that we are so full of joy it is as though we are floating up high in the sky. But where does the number nine come from? We don't know for sure, but one suggestion is that different types of clouds were once ordered by numbers, and cloud nine was a cumulonimbus: the king of all clouds that looks like a giant, fluffy mountain. In a fantasy world, to be floating as high as one of these would make you very happy indeed!

STELLAR

When you look up at the night sky, do you ever wonder how many other people are doing the same, even thousands of miles away? Space is vast, and we are tiny by comparison. Marvelling at the faraway expanse of stars has united us for millennia.

In fact, stars were once believed to shape people's destinies. The playwright William Shakespeare describes his characters Romeo and Juliet as being 'star-crossed lovers' who cannot be together because the stars do not shine favourably upon them. This belief is reflected in many words in English, including 'disaster', which really means 'unlucky star'.

But stars can describe positive things too. When we describe something or someone as 'stellar', which comes from the Latin for star, *stella*, we mean they are brilliant. Stellar people shine like stars.

EDUCATION

When we hear the word 'education' we tend to think of school and university, but it covers so much more than this. Educating ourselves is about growing our personal knowledge and understanding, and expanding our mind and perspective. The word began with a Latin word meaning to 'lead into', because education can move us forward and lead us to new ideas and exciting adventures.

SCIENCE

Science today is often divided into biology, physics and chemistry, and taught with things like microscopes, Bunsen burners and safety goggles. But this word once described all knowledge and learning. It began with a Latin word, *scire*, meaning 'to know'. When it moved into English it meant gaining new knowledge and sharing that knowledge within a community.

Understanding the science of how the natural and physical world works is important for everyone, as this knowledge unites us all and can help us make the world a better place for the future.

LITERATURE

Is there anything that brings us together more than stories? They are the way we connect as human beings. When we read a book, we are forming a bond not just with those around us, but with other people across space and time. Books can start conversations and even friendships. Their stories can teach us that others have experienced the same situations and feelings that we have.

With a book, we are never alone.

The word 'literature' describes the books and words that have been written down over the centuries and which continue to be written and read today. It is fitting that the word comes from the Latin word *littera*, meaning 'letter'. Every book ever written is made up of thousands of letters, which form words that are woven together like golden threads to create a story.

EDUCATION

TSUNDOKU

Are you someone who loves collecting books? The Japanese word *tsundoku* perfectly describes the way many of us buy another book only to add it to a pile of others that we haven't yet read! It is a habit many of us seem to share, but it is not necessarily a bad one. Being surrounded by books, and the hundreds of stories they contain, can give a deep sense of calm and happiness.

LANGUAGE

Try saying the word 'lullaby' out loud. Do you notice what is happening inside your mouth? The tip of your tongue is moving forward to produce the letter L. The tongue is hidden within the word 'language' too, which comes from the Latin *lingua*, meaning 'tongue'. In fact, the word 'tongue' is sometimes used to mean a 'language', such as when we speak our 'mother tongue', which is our first (or native) language.

LIBROCUBICULARIST

When it comes to the places we like to read in, we might choose a cosy armchair, a sunny spot outside or a cool patch under the shade of a huge tree. But some of us like nothing better than reading a good book under the covers! If you're this sort of person, you might like to know that you are a 'librocubicularist' – a person who likes to read in bed.

SCHOOL

The origin of the word 'school' may make you smile, for at its heart is a word meaning 'leisure' or 'enjoyment'. For the ancient Greeks, learning was as much fun as playing games and sport. One of their favourite things to do in their free time was to listen to public lectures. Here they would also meet people and discuss what they had learned.

Their word *skholē*, which became our 'school', meant 'spare time' or 'rest'. Over time, it began to be used for the place where people had these discussions. It's nice to know that 'school' is all about fun and the enjoyment of learning.

ALGEBRA

Algebra is a branch of mathematics that uses letters and symbols to represent different numbers. It can certainly be challenging, and the history of the word is all about putting a difficult puzzle back together! It began with the Arabic word *al-jabr*, which meant 'the reuniting'. It was first used in medicine when doctors would put a patient's broken bones back together in the right places. Perhaps the sight of a lot of complicated symbols reminded ancient mathematicians of a jumbled pile of bones, and that is where they got the name 'algebra' from!

MERAKI

Nothing can be more rewarding than when we put our heart into a project and give it all our energy and love. The Greeks know this as *meraki*, which is about approaching the things we do with passion and spirit.

CALM

The story of the word 'calm' may surprise you. It is based on a Greek word *kauma*, meaning 'heat of the day'. It once described the blistering heat of the midday sun in hot countries, when people would stay indoors and everything became quiet and still. Now it is used to describe a feeling of inner peace and tranquillity. We all find calm in different ways: some of us find it in reading, some by walking or playing sport, and some by being among their family and pets. What brings you inner peace?

SIESTA

In many countries with a hot climate, people go inside and take an afternoon nap to avoid the hottest hours of the day. This rest is known as a 'siesta'.

HUSH

Five hundred years ago, you might have heard someone say the word *Husht!* when they were asking you to be quiet. It is from there that our modern word 'hush' emerged, which means to quieten down. You might say, for example, 'The mother hushes her crying baby with a lullaby.' It can also be used to mean silence itself, when a hush descends and all is still. If you say it out loud, you can hear the soothing, whispering sound of *shhhh*.

SNERDLE

One of the greatest joys in life is snuggling up in the warmth and staying quiet and still. English has lots of words for nestling cosily. One of them is 'snerdling', which even sounds soft and snuggly when you say it aloud. Do you have a favourite place to snerdle?

SERENITY

'Serenity' is a word that sounds as beautiful as its meaning. It is used for all kinds of peaceful situations. A clear and windless day could be described as 'serene', as might someone with a calm, relaxed personality. The word has relatives in many languages, but the root of all of them is the Latin *serenus*, which the ancient Romans used to describe weather that was fair and calm.

FLIBBERTIGIBBET

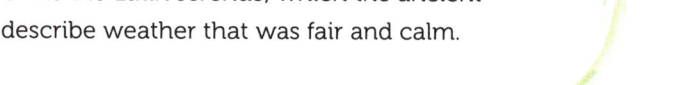

Sometimes it's fun to be the opposite of calm and peaceful – excitable and fizzing! There are certainly lots of words to describe this, including 'flibbertigibbet', which has existed for hundreds of years as a name for someone who is both restless and mischievous. In fact, William Shakespeare used it for a demon or fiend! Today, it is used far more affectionately to mean someone who can never sit still. Don't you find that its bouncy sound is perfect for someone who is forever up and down and rushing about?

SLOOMY

Saturday morning lie-ins, resting in the park beneath a tree or closing your eyes for a moment when reading your favourite book – chances are you have felt 'sloomy' many times in your life. This sleepy word comes from 'sloom', which has existed for over 1,000 years to describe a gentle nap or doze.

JOBLIJOCK

Of course, peace can often be disturbed. Quietness can be broken by the sound of babies crying, dogs barking, brothers and sisters arguing or loud lorries coming down the road. Noises like these can disrupt even the deepest sense of calm. There once was a word to describe these kinds of disturbances: a joblijock. It was originally the name given to a cockerel crowing noisily at dawn, but soon started being used for anything that interrupts our peace and quiet!

LOOSEY-GOOSEY

Do you know someone who is so relaxed that they don't seem to be bothered by anything? One expression for such an easy-going state of mind is 'loosey-goosey'. The first part, 'loosey', suggests someone who is so laid-back they are almost floppy! The second part, 'goosey', was probably chosen simply for its rhyme rather than meaning, as geese aren't known for being particularly relaxed!

HYGGE

Imagine lying under a soft blanket with a cup of steaming hot chocolate in your hand and a fire roaring beside you. Perhaps you are reading a favourite book while breathing in the perfume from a scented candle. Welcome to 'hygge', a word that comes from Danish and describes a cosiness that makes us feel comfortable and content. It is pronounced like 'hoo-guh', and its roots lie in the language of Old Norse, spoken by the Vikings who brought it with them when they invaded British shores between the eighth and eleventh centuries. In their language, 'hygge' meant to 'comfort', and it also gave us the word 'hug'. Hygge describes things around us that hug the senses.

Better still, those things that help us feel 'hygge' can be described with an even warmer, bouncier word: the delightful 'hyggelig'!

ANIMALS

Think of a tiny kitten padding across the kitchen floor, or imagine looking out the window and seeing a cloud of starlings swoop across the sky at dusk. How do these images make you feel? Animals bring us so much joy, and there is a lot of evidence that their company can make us healthier and happier and give us a greater sense of well-being. They allow us to connect with the natural world and step away from our day-to-day worries. Whether they are the pets with which we have a special bond, or the creatures we see in the wild, animals remind us that the world is about so much more than people. They are essential to the harmony of our planet.

Animals were named after the simple fact that they breathe. The root of the word is the Latin *anima*, meaning 'air' or 'breath', which originally described any living being.

INSECT

Insects play a key role in our world, helping to keep everything running in order. Without them, things would be very different. By pollinating lots of our plants, vegetables and fruits, they give us many of the foods we eat and materials we use.

Insects take their name from their shape. If you look closely at any insect, such as an ant or grasshopper, you might notice that its body is divided into three parts. These parts are the head at the top, the thorax in the middle, and the abdomen at the bottom. It was these parts, or 'segments', that inspired the word 'insect', which began as the longer Latin name *animal insectum* that meant 'segmented animal'.

ZOO

A zoo is a place where animals and people come together. 'Zoo' is short for 'zoological', and the scientific study of animals is known as 'zoology'. All these words go back to the Greek *zōion*, meaning 'animal'.

CATERPILLAR

In late spring, you may start to see the beginning of the butterfly's life cycle and notice furry caterpillars crawling up the stem of a plant. Does their appearance remind you of anything? A long time ago, people saw a likeness between caterpillars and other surprising creatures. Our name for this fuzzy animal comes from the Old French word *catepelose*, meaning 'hairy cat'. In French, a caterpillar is now called a *chenille*, which means 'little dog'! Can *you* see a resemblance between caterpillars and cats or dogs?!

When the warm, sunny weather of summer approaches, these caterpillars will transform into colourful monarch, peacock, tortoiseshell and swallowtail butterflies fluttering through the air.

WADDLE

Did you know that groups of animals or birds have different names? These are called 'collective nouns', and many of them date back hundreds of years. We talk about a 'murder of crows', for example, because these dark-coloured birds were once associated with sadness and death. And we describe a flock of starlings as a 'murmuration', because these birds often gather in their thousands and make a soft murmuring sound as they form glorious patterns across the sky. But surely one of the best collective nouns is used for penguins when they are on land and form a 'waddle'.

Have you ever seen

a penguin's

wobbly walk?

Their collective noun

really couldn't be

anything else!

SYMBIOSIS

Animals have very special ways of helping and supporting each other. The word 'symbiosis' describes working together for the good of everyone. In the ocean, the clownfish and the anemone help each other in this way. The anemone shelters the clownfish and even leaves scraps of food for it, while the clownfish scares predators away. It is a simple but essential relationship. Wouldn't it be wonderful if we could all live a symbiotic life?

TRAVEL

There is something incredibly exciting about exploring places we don't yet know; whether it involves travelling thousands of miles or just taking a short journey away from home to somewhere new. Travel allows us to connect with friends and family who live far away, but it also helps us meet and understand other people in the world, who have different traditions and cultures from our own.

We are lucky today to have so many ways to travel, but in medieval times journeys were often made on foot or by horse over rough ground. It is because of this that the first meaning of 'travel' was 'hard work'. It gets worse though, for the word's very beginnings lie in a Latin word linked to torture! Happily, today's travel is much easier than it once was, and it reminds us that there is a world far beyond the boundaries of our own.

TRAILBLAZER

A trailblazer is the first person to achieve something and who sets a path for others to follow. The word originally described someone who made a new track through wild and unexplored places and left a trail behind them. 'Blaze' is the name given to a bright white mark on a tree trunk where a piece of bark has been stripped away. Early explorers would mark trees in this way along their routes. The shining white trunks were used as signposts by others seeking to follow in their footsteps.

FERNWEH

You might know the feeling of homesickness, when you long to be back home after you have been away for a while. But did you know that there is also a word for the opposite: the longing to be far away from home? In German, it is expressed with the beautiful word *Fernweh*, meaning 'far-sickness'. It sums up the feeling of wanting to be somewhere entirely new and different. Haven't we all felt that from time to time?

Astronauts are not just space travellers: they are scientists, engineers and communicators too. But when the idea of exploring the universe beyond Earth began to seem possible in the twentieth century, scientists chose a poetic name for those who might one day be lucky enough to travel into space. 'Astronaut' is based on two Greek words which together mean 'star sailor'. It brings to mind a beautiful image of someone floating across the starry expanse of space, just like sailors exploring the open seas.

TRAVEL

CODDIWOMPLE

'It's not the destination that matters, but the journey.' This popular saying reminds us how much travelling can open our eyes to new experiences and new people. Enjoying the journey to a place can be every bit as important as arriving.

Sometimes, when we set off, we might not even know where we're going! 'Coddiwompling' means heading out on a journey without having an exact destination in mind. Its joyful, skipping sound perfectly captures the idea of setting off on a happy jaunt and seeing where you end up.

HAPPENSTANCE

Sometimes people come together by chance in an unexpected encounter that makes them very happy. In English, this is often known as 'serendipity': a lucky meeting that was completely unplanned. We might also say that such an event was the result of 'happenstance', an old word for coincidence. 'Hap' used to mean 'chance' or 'fate', and can still be found in some words today, including 'perhaps' and 'happy'!

FUTURE

When we look to the future, we think about what we and the world around us might become. The story of the word 'future' reflects that idea of possibility, as its roots are in the Latin *futurus*, meaning 'about to be'. When we hope, we are often imagining what is about to be.

ENVISAGE

Do you sometimes daydream about the future and what lies ahead for you, wondering where life will take you and what adventures await? Anticipating the future is something we all do. To 'envisage' something involves making a picture of it in our heads, even when it doesn't yet exist. 'Visage' is a formal word for 'face', and so to envisage the future is to picture it in one's head and imagine where it will lead.

BETWITTERED

The approach of Christmas or a birthday, the arrival of a new pet or the start of a summer holiday: can you picture that feeling of being overcome with excitement when you know something fun is happening soon and you simply cannot wait? In the nineteenth century, people who were filled with such nervous anticipation were said to be 'betwittered', as though they were chirping away happily and excitedly like birds!

CHERISH

When we look forward to the future, it is also wise to cherish what we already have. To cherish something is to value it. The word comes from the Latin *carus*, meaning 'dear', because when we cherish something, it is special or 'dear' to us.

SISU

Sometimes life can feel hard and unpredictable, and we need all our strength to remember that things will get better. Being able to stay positive and to bounce back from tough times is known as 'resilience': the ability to hold on through difficult moments. In Finland, they know this as *sisu*, which means 'courage' and 'determination', particularly as a community. *Sisu* is a reminder that we are stronger together.

INSPIRE

When we are inspired, we are filled with the desire to do something positive. Those who inspire us give us confidence and the feeling that we can achieve something great. You might even say that they breathe hope into us, and that idea is echoed in the history of the word, which began with the Latin *inspirare*, to 'breathe into'.

I am most inspired when I read, because words are so very powerful. Language is the way we connect with others: it is at the heart of our communities, friendships and relationships. Sometimes all it takes are the right words to inspire people to come together.

I would love it if this book has given you a little bit of inspiration . . .

PRONUNCIATION GUIDE

algebra
[al-je-bra]

altruism
[al-true-ism]

antipelargy
[an-tee-pe-large-y]

armistice
[arm-iss-tiss]

bearn-lufu
[bairn-lufu]

betwittered
[be-twit-ered]

coddiwomple
[coddi-womple]

colloquial
[co-low-qui-al]

conjobble
[con-jobble]

craic
[crack]

envisage
[en-viz-idge]

Fernweh
[fern-vay]

fika
[fee-ka]

flibbertigibbet
[fli-buh-tee-ji-buht]

friluftsliv
[free-loofs-leaf]

gelastic
[gel-astik]

glimmer-gowk
[glimmer-gowk]

hearken
[har-ken]

hygge
[hoo-guh]

joblijock
[job-lee-jock]

karaoke
[ka-ree-o-kee]

koi no yokan
[coy no yo-kahn]

komorebi
[ko-mo-reh-bee]

la passeggiata
[lah pah-seh-gee-arta]

librocubicularist
[li-bro-cu-bic-u-lar-ist]

mensch
[mensh]

meraki
[meh-rah-kee]

philanthropy
[phil-anth-rop-y]

philocaly
[fuh-lock-uh-lee]

pluviophile
[ploo-vee-uh-file]

quiescence
[kwee-es-ens]

salaam
[suh-laam]

shalom
[shuh-lom]

siesta
[cee-es-ta]

simpatico
[sim-pat-icko]

sisu
[see-soo]

snerdle
[sner-dle]

sobremesa
[so-bre-mes-sa]

stound
[stound]

symbiosis
[sim-bi-o-sis]

symphony
[sim-fuh-nee]

tarab
[ta-rab]

tsundoku
[soo-n-dok-u]

wynn
[win]

It is only fitting that a book about sharing was made possible by teamwork. I'm grateful to the wonderful group of people at Puffin, including Phoebe Jascourt, Jess Mackay, Katy Finch, Sally Griffin, and Adam Webling, who have worked in perfect harmony to create something we are all proud of.

I was delighted to work alongside Harriet Hobday once more – her illustrations are a constant source of magic and wonder.

Finally, I dedicate this book to my family, who never cease to remind me of the joy of togetherness.